Brave Mayaki

INTERNET OF PASSIVE INCOME

5 Effective Ways To Make Huge Money While You Sleep

Copyright © 2022 by Brave Mayaki

All rights reserved. No part of this publication may be reproduced, stored or transmitted in any form or by any means, electronic, mechanical, photocopying, recording, scanning, or otherwise without written permission from the publisher. It is illegal to copy this book, post it to a website, or distribute it by any other means without permission.

First edition

This book was professionally typeset on Reedsy
Find out more at reedsy.com

Contents

Introduction 1
Chapter 1 – Ways To Make Money...3
Chapter 2 – Ways To Start Earning Money 5
Chapter 3 – Work area Organizations You Can Use At Home To Bring In Cash..9
Chapter 4 – Information Product Marketing 11
Chapter 5 – Affiliate Programs 14
Chapter 6 – Search Engine Submission Service 18
Conclusion 22
1.
2.
3.
4.
5.
6.
7.

Introduction

Presentation On How the one percent of the world population live....

How do the rich live? We see them on TV playing polo and enjoying a life of ease and comfort. What are they ready to persevere to carry on with that life? Who are these individuals? For what reason do they avoid the drudgery and agony of monetary battle that most appear to persevere? They cover less in charges and procure more with appropriate no work. What are their insider facts?

A superior inquiry isn't "What do they be aware?", yet "What do they do?". I work with affluent individuals. As a corporate chief I have for quite a while. My supervisor is valued at 20 million bucks. His supervisor is valued at 120 million bucks. How would I change my fortune to be more similar to them? All things considered, my feeling of dread needs to go. These men have next to no feeling of dread. This is a base perception. You can NEVER develop rich dreading misfortune or hazard. Individuals become rich by being daring people. Sadly this is the very character that becomes dependent on betting. Rich Financial specialists are speculators and daring people. character is a basic piece of your persona in the event that you hope to develop rich. Sadly bunches of tutoring and lucrative positions put you at the far edge of the range.

Chiefs make their living by being instructed refined and working for security. While these men really do very well, they won't more likely than not ever become rich. Their entirety way of life is in opposition to the gamble taking mindset. One of the main qualities of well off individuals is they have a sound demeanor concerning risk.

The other issue that the poor don't appear to comprehend is the worth of resources and liabilities. Numerous youngsters will say "I would rather not get cash for school", however will go out and burn through $30,000 on another vehicle. An advanced degree can pay you regularly of your functioning life. What resource might you at any point purchase that pays as such? Maybe a value or liabilities portfolio, yet that doesn't pay at regular intervals. The poor don't exploit little enhancements to better the general adequacy of their monetary circumstance. Consistent enhancement prompts a world class status. The following are a few instances of conditions the poor will generally believe are ideal:

(1) No vehicle or possessed transportation
(2) Living in a "modest" neighborhood
(3) Buying a vehicle at a "low-end" vehicle part
(4) Awful Credit "Less expensive not to take care of bills"

Not having a vehicle costs a great deal. People without transportation need to pay for nearly

each spot they go with taxicabs or companions. It is Undeniably more costly to bum rides or pay for a "companion's" gas every step of the way. Modest areas have higher protection rates, and higher assessment rates; NONE of which construct esteem yearly. Buying a vehicle at a low-end part costs definitely more each month than an ordinary buy. At last taking care of your bills is rarely less expensive not. You pay something else for advances, charge cards, and all credit extensions.

The well off make the most of lower loan costs, abundance assemble open doors, resources that form cash esteem, ideal lodging, instructive, and charge conditions. Poor people neglect to exploit these circumstances and with an increasing cost for most everyday items fall farther, and farther   behind.

Chapter 1 - Ways To Make Money....

How would you bring in cash? How would you not let cash utilize you? Very much how about we take the principal question? How would you bring in cash? Here are a few simple ways:

1) W o r k
2) Begin a business
3) Acquire cash
4) Lottery/Bet
5) Wrongdoing

As odd as it sounds, all above are reasonable ways of bringing in cash. The vast majority of the
populace brings in cash through a task. We work for other people. This is a natural, decent and respected way to deal with supporting yourself. The main issue is at times you end up jobless, crushed, and furious. Welcome to a futile way of life!

Beginning a business sounds pleasant. Turn into the supervisor with all the flawless stuff like suits, leader workplaces, and luxurious way of life. This sounds perfect for however long you are effective, and you expect ALL the gamble. We addressed this previously. Intellectually you really want to plan to go through the fire of being a business visionary assuming you have never done this.

Legacy is perfect. You simply need somebody rich to kick the bucket and pass on it to us. This isn't logical and nonrenewable. The cash is continuously running out in the event that you don't make more.

The lottery is essentially NOT going to occur. Betting is outright dumb. Gambling clubs don't fabricate 75 million dollar wellsprings with the cash they lost to benefactors.

The constants in bringing in cash are readiness, conservation and sweat.

The readiness we'll call the cash trap. Readiness bases on the business develop, the advertising activity and the completion. Productivity is critical. Protection implies that your business should save its worth.

Esteem inserted as hard resources, or monetary instruments have for quite some time been utilized for esteem protection. Conservation of significant worth is re-venture. Re-venture is business building. Sweat is the evident expense of buying and maintaining a business. The vast majority of the dreams about running and possessing your own business blur when the independently employed understand that when they don't work, they don't eat. This is the difficult work that no one enjoys to discuss. Fruitful proprietors are steady, restrained and centered individuals. They show up on Saturday or Sunday, occasions, and essentially regular.

Most business has passage boundaries, the base expense of speculation. With the time of PCs has come new organizations like web showcasing, work area organizations, and other advanced organizations. It is important that business visionaries exploit robotization. Barely any business structures don't include communication, high passage hindrances (huge speculations to begin) and different hardships. MOST customary physical organizations include the speculation of thousands of dollars, frequently with no business preparing or tutoring in the field of business.

The fact that fits the accompanying depiction makes an astonishing business one:

1) Low or no speculation
2) Requires pretty much nothing/low time speculation
3) Requires not many/no representatives
4) Gives a Sustainable type of revenue
5) Administrations are Preferred over merchandise, as administrations are limitlessly inexhaustible, items arrive at a deals development level and decline

Chapter 2 - Ways To Start Earning Money

Data Business visionary

A data deal is a strong, modest and compelling approach to bringing in cash. It is the absolute most useful asset for web deals that exists. Business visionaries can make Large number of dollars each day offering data to other people. Here are a few vital variables around here:

1) Item Advancement Time spans
2) Item Life cycle
3) Site Costs (Keep them low and packaged)
4) Advertising Strategies
5) Rundown building
6) Test Promoting Procedures
7) Item Cloning
8) Law of Business variety
9) Income arranging

We will dive into every one of these techniques and how to utilize them to fabricate a

fruitful Web promoting business, E-bay business, Google Ad-sense, On-line Travel Planner, Traffic Affiliate, and Web index accommodation administration. You might consider how all of this can help in the wide range of various regions. The center business standards apply to anything that business you get into. We should seriously investigate E-bay:

E-bay Business Arranging

- Item Improvement Time period: N/A
- Item Life-cycle: 30-120 days
- Site Costs: 2-6%of each and every buy
- Promoting Procedures: Advertising strategies for outside sites can be troublesome. Connections to your site are not open and self-evident. E-inlet boycotts merchants that market outside destinations without purchasing a store.
- Normal buy: 0.01- $30.00

- Client Rundown Building: Client list expanding on E-bay is non-Existent. Clients are not really connected with the dealer, and in the event that you put them on a rundown without approval you are spamming your clients.
- Test Promoting Procedures: The An dale E-bay tool-set (http://www.andale.com) is extremely great, and completely utilitarian.
- Item Cloning: It is exceptionally simple to find, and clone a fruitful item on E-bay with the exploration item. Item cloning is a savvy and simple method for bringing in cash quick. With the An dale device, you can find, disengage and duplicate an item quicker than you can sniffle.
- Law of Business Variety: Consistently consolidate organizations, so that during times of monetary pressure, some business will in any case create, similar to stocks in a portfolio. E-commerce is a pleasant business to have on the grounds that it produces consistent pay absent a lot of time inclusion. Income Arranging: You Should design the following month's income today. Your business requests you get a schedule and sow monetary seeds for the following month farther.

E-bay is most certainly a business you can bring in cash on while you rest. You should simply make (not buy and exchange) 20-40 items and sell them on E-bay. These should be items you produce yourself that Can't be purchased in a standard store. These items ought to be extremely modest to deliver, modest to transport, and recorded as efficiently as could be expected. After your underlying deals you really want to convey second offers. The subsequent offers will bring extra income. A few instances of productive things available to be purchased on E-bay are:

1. Data Items (Paper)
2. Extraordinary Sauces and Blends (Generally water)
3. Printing/Composing Administrations (Administration)
4. Automobiles (Fix stalled vehicles)
5. Custom Administrations

These are things you can get as efficiently as could be expected, add a significant markup and afterward exchange. E-bay can be a basic piece of your portfolio, however its significant restriction is that E-bay items will generally sell modest, and assuming you want to begin a full-time business you need to sell 50-120 E-bay things each week to get by at it. This is definitely not a wonderful possibility. Your normal everyday employment might be a lot more straightforward than this. Presently, we should check out again at the rundown, this time with somewhat "better" view:

- Data Items (Paper)
- Printing/Composing Administrations (Administration)
- Custom Administrations

Sack any E-bay business that includes a production network if you have any desire to bring in cash while you rest. Inventory network the board is intense. At the point when your computerized optics sell on E-bay on Tuesday, you don't need them sitting on a dock across the US. Center around administrations you can furnish from home on a Saturday with simply your nearby assets. E-bay worldwide is a book composed simply on this specific subject. Buying abroad, paying obligation, and managing individuals in different nations who might screw you isn't charming. Stick to what you know and simplify the framework. KISS, "Keep It Straightforward" is a typical expression. E-bay is a brilliant business that could make them inhabit the mailing station, going through hours wrapping and assembling bundles or it very well may be a straightforward $1000 each month professional mine that requires 2 hours of the week. It is your decision.

Presently how about we recap how to streamline E-bay:

1. Make your own items.
2. Deal with your income through arrangement ahead of time.
3. Utilize the An dale apparatuses (http://www.andale.com) to clone fruitful items and make them advantageous for you
4. Center around items that are in the $20 - $40 territory, less expensive items require a ton of significant investment. You maintain that your business should merit your time.
5. E-bat brings in cash for you 24 hours of the day, with little exertion if we need to advance it.

All in all, E-bay is an extremely integral asset whenever utilized in an upgraded configuration, and it tends to be areas of strength for an in the business portfolio.

Chapter 3 - Work area Organizations You Can Use At Home To Bring In Cash

The following are a few instances of work area organizations you can use at home to bring in cash:

Resume composing
E-sound
Web Data Advertising
Long-lasting Tourists....

There are a great deal of advantages to living and working external your day to day climate. It is extremely challenging to expand your gamble resistance while you are "caught" by your current way of life. Frequently financial specialists "find" themselves when laid off. You might have to step outside your life to go a higher level.

A great many people can't imagine themselves venturing outside their ways of life since we are so very much molded to go to a task. Consider it, you are prepared to get going "some place" on a timetable your whole life. In kindergarten, kids are molded to get up and live on a timetable starting there on. Genuine money managers don't have an unbending timetable. They procure their direction by offsetting risk with remuneration, one of which is individual flexibility. What is your opportunity worth? Frequently we ask would could it be that the effective realize that we don't. The response isn't anything. The distinction between the finance manager and us is that he will acknowledge the gamble or intense approach to just barely survive and we will not. We beseech you to bring your boldness. Gather your boldness and come an extended get-away with me for a second.....

Imagine....

You have chosen to follow your deepest longings. You have left your place of employment and returned home. You want a business you can run efficiently with practically no speculation. On the 15-twentieth you have more than $1100 in bills due. How will you respond? You really want a productive vehicle to bring in cash and you really want to bring in cash now! You need to step outside your life once more. Imagine a scenario in which you had a vehicle to bring in cash and you gave it all that you needed to get it moving. Imagine a scenario in which you took care of it with a similar impressive skill you do you work, with a similar planning and concern. What might that business be worth to you?!! There are a ton of alternate ways of venturing outside your life. You could venture out to an unfamiliar country for motivation. Following are a few objections and what they have been noted for by and large:

Egypt - Learning and Training

Paris - Food, Wine, Craftsmanship

Italy - Food, Wine, Craftsmanship, Government, Religion Japan - Business, History

Britain - History, Learning and Training

Chapter 4 - Information Product Marketing

Data items are useful assets. On the off chance that E-bay is the "Compact disc" of your business portfolio, data items are the stocks. They are either hot or they are cold. Data items are amazing assets that basically "make" cash. You set up a framework that sets you up as the master. From that point, you sell units, tapes, books, and so on about the subject of your business. However, you really help need definitely showcasing procedure to sell these things. Here are a few basic focuses about selling data items on-line:

1. The typical individual sees an item multiple times prior to getting it on-line.
2. The premise of any promoting program is redundancy. A single shot bargains don't work. This is much of the time why fliers and momentary paper promotions yield terrible outcomes.
3. You really want to isolate the arbitrary eyewitnesses or guests from qualified and intrigued purchasers. You want to begin a mailing list, and convey pamphlets. This illuminates your certified purchasers that you are there and keeps them intrigued by your program.
4. Make the way for your public. Request that they give input and talk about the item at length with them. Cause your vendors to feel that you care about them and that your item IS advantageous.
5. Make your pamphlets amiable, don't give your endorsers the hard sell, sell delicately and discuss yourself and your existence with your expected clients.
6. Work WITH your clients. You ought to converse with disappointed clients and get their perspective on your item.

The following is a rundown of beneficial on-line items for data deals:

1. Home Organizations
2. Clinical Items

3. Sex Items (we don't suggest it)
4. Testing Items
5. Legitimate Items
6. Cooking/Food Items
7. Betting Items (we don't suggest it)
8. Gaming Items

Data promoting is a business that has extremely clear goals and steps with regards to selling. A fundamental outline is accessible underneath;

| Buyer's |
| Qualified And Interested Pool of Potential Customers |
| General Public |

The main highlight recollect is the means by which to move individuals starting with one piece of the pyramid then onto the next and eventually to the purchaser's region. The mailing rundown and correspondence is the strategy for help for this business. At the point when potential purchasers answer advertisements, you Must be there to converse with them. Utilizing administrations like replying mail or "virtual workplaces" just mask what your identity is. You are selling your business, so converse with your clients and sell your item yourself. The vast majority realize it is a little activity. Quit taking cover behind your site or ad, just huge retailers and partnerships can do that.

List of most well-known botches data merchants make on the web:

1. Selling data items you are not a specialist on
2. Refusal to converse with or face clients one-on-one
3. Inappropriate web composition
4. Making a facade to take cover behind with 1-800 numbers, and dead telephone lines 5. Inability to connect with the client straightforwardly and circle back to leads

You can't sell data you are not a specialist on. It goes over in the data item. Your clients will request discounts. Your discourse and messages won't persuade. This is a bad dream. Try not to attempt this!

Declining to converse with potential clients is a passing nail. You are doing this since you are giving a trash item. A solid item has a decent history, low or presently returns and you can converse with clients subsequently. On the off chance that your item is disgraceful or you are uncertain, offer it first and try things out. Unfortunate client criticism will obliterate your standing. Testing the market with any market prior to selling it is better. This is a basic point you essentially should comprehend.

Inappropriate web composition is likewise a typical error. Kindly note clients could do without to make a ton of snaps on sites. This implies your pamphlet should accumulate data in what Google calls the "hot zone" of the screen. Clients ought to have the option to include their email address without extra snaps. Clients ought to have the option to include their addresses, buy and play out any or other basic business exercises with at least extra snaps. Entrepreneurs need to awaken.

Individuals will burn through 10 minutes on Ford.com sorting this stuff out. They won't do it on *simple testing.com.* Allow them to buy, pursue pamphlets and anything very quickly in the wake of visiting your site. You will find success, I guarantee. We should recap these things:

1. Set your mailing list join in the Goggle "hot zone" of the screen
2. Put your buy connect in the Google "hot zone" of the screen
3. Continuously make a mailing list join

Making a facade to take cover behind makes disarray and "space" among yourself and your clients. For example, clients answer by calling your 800 number with live administrators yet you email them from a yahoo address! That is crazy. Veneers should be finished to work, and they only from time to time roused trust. Trust is precisely exact thing you are attempting to construct. You ought to just not do this. Converse with your clients one-on-one and watch the deals come in.

Following up leads and making a modified reaction for requests is key for deals. Call your kin and let them call you. This appears to be in opposition to the enormous deals mindset. Trust is the foundation for web deals. Make the way for requests and you make the way for deals. It is just straightforward. When you assemble this trust, you'll have the option to convey one email to you list at 7 pm, and in the first part of the day when you awaken, you'll have $1000 in your Pay-pal account. It is just basic.

Chapter 5 - Affiliate Programs

We will utilize the term offshoot projects to allude to all partner programs other than Google. Some offshoot programs are bundled like those at commission intersection. In the event that you have not known about cj.com, it is the web address of commission intersection. Commission intersection is a subsidiary "Mecca". There you can find Master-card programs, land, advances, and so on. These individuals have some expertise in selling items on- line for different organizations. The absolute most lucrative member lead programs are recorded underneath:

- Countrywide
- LowerMyBills.com
- Unfamiliar Charge card Organizations Chase Manhattan Bank

These projects pay for leads. Leads are basically web surfers that finish up structures for their site. You post the structure on your site, and when structures are finished, you get a really look at via the post office. Member programs are extremely hot at the present time. Getting clients to finish up structures can be extremely difficult, and obviously there are a few clever deceives you want to be aware.

Frequently the compensation per lead can be very high, for example a few projects can pay $32.00 per finished structure, and Master-card organizations can pay $150 per endorsed charge card application. Getting clients to finish up Master-card applications can be incredibly rewarding!

Here are a normally utilized strategies to get clients to finish up structures:

1. Offer an unconditional gift (this is a similar strategy utilized in shopping centers)
2. Stack your applications for a "pleasant" gift (this can at times net as much as $500 per individual with great credit)
3. Utilize a mailing rundown of confided in assets to get structures finished up

4. Place the structures in local area sites where guests understand agreeable in filling structure
5. Make "free stuff" sites where guests come hoping to accomplish a little work get something free of charge
6. Target market your items by offering free Cd's to music sweethearts, and so forth
7. Spread your payments across sites focusing on high and low commission thing putting together your promoting with respect to client premium versus your requirement for cash

The most extravagant member programs expect clients to become leads for major
organizations. Different projects essentially expect clients to tap on a connection on the site. By a long shot the greatest of these projects is Google's compensation per-click program. Hurray has likewise begun a comparative program, yet it isn't quite as full grown as Google. Many, numerous more modest projects exist asserting they pay more per click than Google yet you want to look out for a few major hindrances. That's what numerous advertisers imagine assuming they get to the highest point of a web crawler in a class they will get rich. It essentially doesn't work that way. Frequently traffic to a site just proselytes at a pace of 1-3% to Adsense clicks. This pattern is valid with other compensation per-click programs also. Nothing can be more important than pertinent advertisements spilling to your subsidiary site. Web position is vital, however promotion importance is the second, basic piece. How great does it be the second site on Yippee, in South Carolina business which gets a normal of 6,000 hits each month when, all your Google advertisements are tied in with banking? Your connections won't ever get clicked. The equivalent is valid with other compensation per-click programs.

Google Affiliate Program Advertising

A Google program changes stunningly in its income. It's anything but a decent essential business yet a magnificent optional revenue source. Google ought to be piggy-upheld on a solid traffic affiliate and structure based offshoot business. Client clicks are too irregular to possibly be a solid revenue source. Google is an astounding "sauce" program since it takes care of straightforwardly from the traffic your site as of now creates. Google snaps can be a "side-effect" of a generally working business and it costs you nothing to attempt. We have all heard bits of gossip about individuals making $15,000 each day from Google clicks. Google pay is a "irregular walk". It moves in an irregular example whenever diagrammed on an outline. This isn't great as an essential type of revenue. Google likewise pays provided that your presentation meets specific necessities. This is another restriction that must be survived. However, we have designed a philosophy to mix each of the qualities of Google with the qualities of different projects. Google can supply you with one more really look at via the post office for a solitary business. Google promotions require no extra upkeep, so whenever they are implanted in your site, you really want not irritate them once more. In the event that you mix Google, Data Promoting, Subsidiary Showcasing and Traffic exchanging into one business. It would seem to be the outline underneath. The coolest piece of this hypothesis is that it truly is overall a similar business.

Presently we should recap how this cooperates. You can construct and test market your data items and sell them quickly on E-bay. This is one new pay pathway. Items that sell well on E-bay could be moved to their own site and once more (same item) sold as another data item. As an autonomous item it could sell for in excess of multiple times what it sold for on E-narrows. Data items can acquire sums as high as $1000 per thing. Data items and E-bay structure the foundation of the pyramid on the grounds that their pay potential could without much of a stretch supplant your work, and deals can be ordinary and reliable

These two things are not traffic reliant however much they are "interest" subordinate. Their deals will depend on your standing on E-bay and on different types of correspondence.Partner deals and being a traffic affiliate can be an exceptionally high income business however it is reliant of web traffic which is irregular. At $100 per finished structure this is explosive, yet the irregular component of web traffic makes it a preferred optional revenue stream over an essential one. You can decisively put your site; you can streamline it for Google and Hurray, and have moderate achievement. Your assumptions ought to be connected to your traffic enhancement capacity and site planning. You really want to likewise be aware of the way that each associate program pays in an unexpected way. A few deals you make this month may not be accessible for 30 after 40 days.

At last you ought to think about your Google Adsense business. Google income can fluctuate fiercely. It is a fantastic "sauce" business. Presently we should survey this pyramid in real life and investigate its outcomes. The information underneath is genuine monetary information from a data items advertiser.

Chapter 6 - Search Engine Submission Service

You can bring in cash by setting up your own web crawler accommodation and page advancement administration. You can buy this code for pennies at script buying regions on scriptlance.com or hotscripts.com. Web search tool accommodation scripts essentially take client input and submit them to web index administrations. You can likewise charge Large expenses for page improvement. Certain individuals pay as much as $1000 to have their pages streamlined for web search tool accommodation. Most expenses for web search tool accommodation are little, yet page customization for accommodation charges are much of the time huge. These administrations are correlative and ought to be packaged for greatest monetary effect. Here are a few ways to begin this help:

1. Overture.com offers free devices for enhancing pages
2. Web crawler entries can offer a great deal of rehash business making a rundown of clients and offering motivators that can without much of a stretch invigorate pay
3. A portion of these contents are FREE, look for them industriously

This business can net you about $1000 per upgraded project and $10-$70 per

web indexes accommodation. The benefit potential here is very high site improvement (Website optimization) can be as basic adding the suggestion idea words to the catchphrase contents segment of a page. A few incredible sites to visit are recorded underneath to assist you with this help:

- www.google.com
- www.hotscripts.com
- www.scriptlance.com
- www.elance.com (www.upwork.com)
- www.50lycos.com
- www.scripts.com

This business offers a great deal of rehash business potential. Catchphrases change in their significance over the long haul. So when you do an enhancement for a client, you can call them up in 3-6 months and ask to "re-optimize" their pages. Assuming pages are doing great in their classification and clients are acquiring great, they will absolutely love to pay your charge in the future for your administration.

As a web hits traffic affiliate you can procure sizable pay by selling traffic from your page to create traffic to another site. A few sites pay excellent cash per hit to divert or utilize pop-ups to produce hits. Two excellent administrations for this are:

1. http://www.maxvisits.com/affiliate program.HTML
2. http://mthitssupply.com/

You could without much of a stretch exploit these administrations and create additional month to month pay from your high volume sites. Exchanging your traffic has a drawback, it diverts clients from your sites. You should make certain to keep up with client interest inside your own web advantages so your deals don't diminish. Assuming you notice, there is another packaging methodology that could be utilized utilizing Adsense, web hits resales, and web search tool entries. Every one of the three of these organizations depend vigorously on volume. You can fabricate another benefit pyramid using an on-line travel service as a base. The travel service, in view of a physical idea like a club or affiliation could turn out a steady revenue through bunch connection and use. The web search tool accommodation and site design improvement administration could shape a less solid pay level that could sizably add to proprietor's month to month spending plan. The top layer again could be the irregular pay base of Google Adsense and web hits resales. This irregular layer turns out revenue inclusion in an income spread that changes fiercely.

These layers of pay can give consistent income streams that could undoubtedly supplant your everyday work. The travel service takes in pieces in the $100-$300 territory, the web crawler accommodation administration will likely less habitually give your business portfolio knocks in the $30-$75 territory, while the hits resale from a higher volume site and research Adsense can frame a magnificent type of extra pay for an online business.

A month to month profile for an effective advertiser could seem to be the accompanying:

Advertiser Z

On-line Travel Service Web crawler Administration and Search engine optimization Google and Hits Resales

$4700

$3800

$ 10 0 0

Pay for the profile's month to month all out equivalent $9500. Advertisers need to take a gander at their general procedures and utilize a packaged system that exploits those assets the advertiser as of now has accessible. The profile above thinks about that the advertiser has traffic in overflow. The prior profile was not centered around traffic but rather generally on item fixation, improvement and imagination. The peruser should peer inside himself/herself and ask what his/her most prominent assets are. The situations introduced here are only a couple of potential situations. Packaging and systems are the center component in exploiting any traffic that enters your site. We should investigate a few exercises that you can bring in cash off of at whatever point a surfer enters your site. A potential guest could:

1. Purchase an item
2. Snap a connection
3. Leave the site by means of another connection
4. Enter a spring up on your site to go to another site
5. Download programming
6. Complete a data structure
7. Complete and apply for an advance or MasterCard
8. Plan an outing or excursion or another action

Each thing recorded above is an action you can be paid for. Each action can happen without your immediate inclusion. Packaging these exercises allows clients more opportunities to bring in cash for you. Shut your eyes and consider it. I stay with your site and I see the screen. There are 15 connections on your site. The connections on the screen are exit and passage connects to different sites. Each thing on the screen is associated with bring in cash for your business somehow or another. This ought to be your objective. Your sites ought to be stacked with monetary open doors similarly that a rancher sows seeds in a field.

Kindly recall the business you are building is resource rich. Each dollar you contribute today is potential benefit tomorrow. You should separate the most extreme worth of your business consistently. Your site creates traffic, client clicks, item orders, and constructs your contact list 24 hours out of each day. It is basic that the individual who involves the web as a type of revenue know the genuine worth of web assets. Web index position and direct requests are just pointers. A genuine money manager realizes that achievement lies in the separating of greatest worth from all web assets. For individuals who began in the web a long time back, it was impractical to be paid for approaching and cordial traffic. They recall a web that was totally unregulated, unpolished, unintelligent, non-dynamic and practically inept. Today you can arrange a hot pizza through the web. The web has changed, and it has turned into a mother lode. Advertisers should be more intelligent and savvier to bring in cash on the web. Everybody has known about individuals who make $5.00 each day on Google. Would you like to be one of these individuals? We don't really.

Packaged systems exploit all around planned sites with layered income gulfs.

Obviously a very much planned site with moderate traffic is resource rich. It is your occupation as an advertiser to get out there and concentrate that worth. In the event that you set up these devices, in a keenly layered style, you can set up a situation where checks come to you via the post office and your PayPal account tops off quicker than a liquor's shot glass.

Conclusion

The things in this guide are a strong tool set that sets out numerous monetary open doors for you.

It is our most profound expectation that these devices when appropriately utilized will give you the achievement that they have managed the cost of us for over 7 years. In the event that you follow these ideas not exclusively will you bring in cash while you rest, your fantasies will be loaded up with gold!

Thanks again for taking the time to examine our materials.

www.ingramcontent.com/pod-product-compliance
Lightning Source LLC
Chambersburg PA
CBHW070322220526
45465CB00013B/2183